POSITIONS ON THE TEAM

POSITIONS IN BASKETBALL

AMY B. ROGERS

PowerKiDS press

New York

Published in 2023 by The Rosen Publishing Group, Inc.
29 East 21st Street, New York, NY 10010

Portions of this work were originally authored by Ryan Nagelhout and published as *Basketball: Who Does What?* All new material in this edition was authored by Amy B. Rogers.

Editor: Katie Kawa
Book Design: Michael Flynn

Photo Credits: Cover and interior (basketball) Kirill Demchenko/Shutterstock.com; (series jersey texture) Kwangmoozaa/Shutterstock.com; cover (wood floor texture) ampcool/Shutterstock.com; cover (basketball play) Dejan Popovic/Shutterstock.com; p. 5 (main) Alex Kravtsov/Shutterstock.com; p. 5 (inset) https://commons.wikimedia.org/wiki/File:James_Naismith_at_Springfield_College_circa_1920.jpg; pp. 7, 19 Monkey Business Images/Shutterstock.com; pp. 8, 15 photoyh/Shutterstock.com; p. 9 Vasyl Shulga/Shutterstock.com; p. 10 landmarkmedia/Shutterstock.com; p. 11 Auttapol Sangsub/Shutterstock.com; p. 13 Ververidis Vasilis/Shutterstock.com; p. 17 Christopher Halloran/Shutterstock.com; p. 18 Master1305/Shutterstock.com; p. 21 Oleksii Sidorov/Shutterstock.com; p. 23 wavebreakmedia/Shutterstock.com; p. 25 AP Photo/Marcio Jose Sanchez; p. 26 eurobanks/Shutterstock.com; p. 27 bbernard/Shutterstock.com; p. 28 ACHPF/Shutterstock.com; p. 29 salajean/Shutterstock.com.

Library of Congress Cataloging-in-Publication Data

Names: Rogers, Amy B.
Title: Positions in basketball / Amy B. Rogers.
Description: New York : Powerkids Press, 2023. | Series: Positions on the team | Includes glossary and index.
Identifiers: ISBN 9781538386972 (pbk.) | ISBN 9781538386996 (library bound) | ISBN 9781538386989 (6pack) | ISBN 9781538387009 (ebook)
Subjects: LCSH: Basketball--Juvenile literature.
Classification: LCC GV885.1 R64 2023 | DDC 796.323--dc23

Manufactured in the United States of America

Some of the images in this book illustrate individuals who are models. The depictions do not imply actual situations or events.

CPSIA Compliance Information: Batch #CSPK23. For Further Information contact Rosen Publishing, New York, New York at 1-800-237-9932.

CONTENTS

ON THE COURT

Basketball has changed a lot over time. In the earliest days of the sport, there were no rules for how many players could be on the court at one time. Some early games even had 50 people from each team on the court together! Today, though, things look a lot simpler, with five players per team on the court.

These five players often play different positions, and each position has a special job that goes along with it—from scoring points to getting rebounds. What are these different positions, and how do they work together to help their team win? Read on to find out!

PLAYING IN THE PROS

Basketball is a sport for everyone! The most talented male basketball players in the United States and Canada play in the National Basketball Association (NBA). The most talented women play in the Women's National Basketball Association (WNBA). It takes a lot of hard work to become a **professional**, or pro, basketball player.

JAMES NAISMITH

THINK FAST!

BASKETBALL IS BELIEVED TO HAVE BEEN INVENTED IN SPRINGFIELD, MASSACHUSETTS, IN 1891 BY A MAN NAMED JAMES NAISMITH.

Basketball players have to have a strong understanding of what their role, or job, on the court is.

BASKETBALL BASICS

A basketball game is played between teams of five players, and there are five basic positions those players are grouped into. Players often stand in certain places on the court depending on which position they play. The basic positions are divided between two different areas: the frontcourt and the backcourt.

The frontcourt includes the players that usually play closest to the net. The **post** player, or center, plays closest to the net. The power forward also plays very close to the net, while the small forward moves around more. The backcourt is made up of guards—usually a point guard and a shooting guard.

GETTING STARTED

If you're interested in trying out any of the positions on a basketball team for yourself, there are many ways to get started. You can shoot hoops with your friends at a park in your neighborhood or in someone's backyard if they have a basketball hoop set up. Many pro basketball players started playing on school teams or Amateur Athletic Union (AAU) travel teams.

THINK FAST!

SOMETIMES BASKETBALL GAMES ARE PLAYED WITH ONLY THREE PLAYERS ON EACH TEAM. THIS IS CALLED 3-ON-3, OR 3X3, BASKETBALL.

The five basketball players who begin a game are often called the starting five.

THE POINT GUARD

Different sports often have one player who runs the offense. In basketball, that position is the point guard. A point guard runs scoring plays on offense and makes a lot of passes to teammates spread out on the floor.

Stephen Curry is one of the most successful point guards in NBA history. He has also played on the U.S. Olympic team.

THREE-POINT SHOOTERS

Point guards sometimes get the chance to take three-point shots, often called 3-pointers. These are shots taken from behind a certain line on the court that are worth three points instead of two. In 2021, Stephen Curry, a point guard for the Golden State Warriors, set the record for most 3-pointers in a career.

If they see an opening, point guards will drive toward the net to shoot. Other times, they'll pass to other players, then stay in the backcourt and be ready to get back on defense. Whether they're passing or shooting, point guards need to be fast and smart so they can make quick plays. Point guard is a very important position!

THINK FAST!

POINT GUARDS OFTEN HOLD UP THEIR HAND TO SIGNAL WHAT PLAY THEY WANT TO RUN. THEIR TEAMMATES KNOW WHAT THE DIFFERENT HAND SIGNALS MEAN.

THE BEST SHOOTER

A shooting guard is often the best shooter on their team. They're able to score all over the court. Shooting guards must always be ready to take the shot, so they should be able to think fast and shoot **accurately** from many different spots on the court.

AIR JORDAN

Michael Jordan is known as one of the greatest basketball players of all time. He most famously played shooting guard and was a superstar for the Chicago Bulls in the NBA during the 1980s and 1990s. He won six **championships** with Chicago and was known for his impressive scoring ability and his ability to dunk the basketball. That's how he got his nickname–Air Jordan!

Point guards usually have better ball-handling, or dribbling and passing, skills than shooting guards. However, both need to be good at dribbling and moving around defenders. Shooting guards need to get to spots on the floor they know they can make shots from. Getting open to take the shot is an important part of a shooting guard's job.

THINK FAST!

SHOOTING GUARDS OFTEN SCORE A LOT USING JUMP SHOTS. THESE ARE SHOTS TAKEN WHILE JUMPING, WITH THE BALL BEING RELEASED AT THE PEAK OF THE JUMP.

Shooting guards have to practice different kinds of shots and different angles for shooting.

SMALL FORWARD FACTS

Compared to guards, small forwards often aren't small. However, they're often smaller than centers and power forwards. Small forwards are usually the best all-around player on their team. They can play both close to and away from the net.

Small forwards need to shoot, but they also need to use their size to track down shots they or another player missed. This is called rebounding. When an offensive player gets a rebound, their team has another chance to score points.

Some small forwards fill **specific** roles on their team. They might be a defensive specialist or used more as a shooter.

THE WINGS

The small forward and shooting guard are sometimes called the wings. This is because they often play near the sidelines, or sides, of the court instead of going up the middle of the court. The wings are often versatile players. This means they're good at many different things.

THINK FAST!

THE SMALL FORWARD ON A BASKETBALL TEAM IS ALSO SOMETIMES CALLED THE "THREE."

Small forwards often have to battle against players from the other team while waiting for a rebound. Everyone wants the ball and the chance to score!

USING THEIR POWER

Power forwards are often taller and stronger than small forwards. In fact, they're usually the second-tallest and second-strongest player on a team. Power forwards need to do a few things very well. They must rebound on offense and defense. Power forwards also set screens to free up other players on offense.

Power forwards score points themselves too. They usually take shots near the basket or in the space between the **key** and the three-point line. This is called a midrange shot. A power forward with a good jump shot is a big **asset** to their team.

SETTING A SCREEN

Sometimes a power forward is at their best when they're not moving at all! A screen is a play where the forward reaches a certain spot on the court and stops moving. This gets in the way of a defender who's chasing the player with the ball. It also lets a player with the ball run a certain play.

THINK FAST!

A POWER FORWARD OFTEN PLAYS WITH THEIR BACK TO THE BASKET SO THEY CAN FACE THE PLAYER WITH THE BALL.

Basketball can be a tough sport to play! Power forwards use their size and strength to help their team win.

AT THE CENTER OF IT ALL

Basketball players are often relatively tall, and the center is almost always the tallest player on their team. They take any tip-offs in a game. They play closest to the hoop, taking passes from the point guard and dribbling their way into the key. Most often, centers match up against other centers in a part of the court known as the post.

In the post, centers try to make the defender back up so they can get close enough to the basket to dunk. Centers are great at scoring on shots close to the basket that are most likely to go in. These are called high-percentage shots.

TAKING THE TIP-OFF

A basketball game always starts with a tip-off. This is when a jump ball happens to start or restart play. A jump ball is a method of putting the ball into play in which the **referee** tosses the ball in the air between two opposing players. Then, the players jump up and try to gain possession, often by tapping the ball to their teammate.

The sixth player can often play different positions well. They're sometimes even more talented than starting players—and they may play for much longer in the game.

THINK FAST!

THE NBA AND WNBA BOTH GIVE OUT AWARDS, OR PRIZES, FOR THE BEST SIXTH PLAYER AT THE END OF EVERY SEASON.

Starting the game on the bench doesn't mean a player isn't important. Every player on a basketball team can help their team win.

DEFENSIVE BASKETBALL

Players at every position on the basketball court need to be able to play defense in addition to trying to score points. They match up against their **opponents** and do their best to stop them from scoring points. Defending a player in basketball is called guarding them.

Guarding talented offensive players isn't easy! Defenders need to have quick **reflexes** to **react** to what an opposing player does while dribbling. The best defensive players can guard another player one-on-one, or without help from their teammates. However, teamwork is an important part of basketball, and players at every position help each other when they need it.

STOPPING THE STARS

Some basketball teams have a special player who just plays defense. This kind of player is called a "defensive stopper" or just a "stopper." They may not have the best skills on offense, but they're usually the best defensive player on the team. They typically stay on the bench until they're needed to stop the opposing team's star players.

THINK FAST!

AS SOON AS THE OPPOSING TEAM GETS POSSESSION OF THE BASKETBALL, THE OTHER FIVE PLAYERS NEED TO HUSTLE, OR RUN FAST, TO PLAY DEFENSE.

It's fun to score points and take shots, but playing strong defense is also an important part of being a good basketball player.

DIFFERENT KINDS OF DEFENSES

There are different ways to play defense on the basketball court. Person-to-person defense is when every player is given an opposing player to guard at all times. In men's basketball games, this is called man-to-man defense. This kind of defense matches players based on their size and skill.

A zone defense gives each player a certain area of the floor to guard. Offensive players move in and out of these zones trying to shift defensive players and get chances to shoot. Coaches might plan to use one kind of defense based on their opponent, but they might change from one to the other in the same game!

GETTING INTO POSITION

Most defenses work best when they are given time to set up. Players get into position on their defensive side of the court and wait for the offensive team to attack the basket. Defenses can be successful farther down the court, but the team on offense often has a better chance of finding ways through the defensive players.

THINK FAST!

ZONE DEFENSES ARE NAMED FOR WHERE PLAYERS ARE SET UP ON THE COURT. FOR EXAMPLE, IN A 2-3 ZONE, TWO PLAYERS GUARD THE FRONTCOURT AND THREE GUARD THE BACKCOURT.

The players on a basketball team are important, and so is the coach. A coach decides what kind of defense to play and draws up offensive plays too.

MIXING SKILLS

Many basketball players have tried playing more than one position over the course of their career. Some players are moved from position to position throughout their time on the court. For example, a "swingman" is someone who can swing, or move, between the two and three—shooting guard and small forward—positions on the court.

Some players don't fit the mold of one specific position, but their style of play combines skills from different positions. These hybrid, or mixed, positions in basketball include the point forward. This kind of player combines the skills of a point guard and a forward.

KING JAMES

LeBron James is a successful example of a basketball player with many different strengths and skills. He's played guard and forward positions throughout his career, and he's been called a point forward at times. "King James" is considered one of the game's all-time greats, and it's because he can do many different things to help his team win.

THINK FAST!

A SWINGMAN IS SOMETIMES CONSIDERED A HYBRID POSITION TOO.

Some basketball players are talented at many different aspects, or parts, of the game. LeBron James is one of those players.

PLAYING BY THE RULES

No matter what position you play on a basketball team, you have to follow the rules. Fouls are called by officials when players make contact in a way that's against the rules. Bumping a player to the ground, hitting their hand while they dribble, and pushing someone out of the way are three ways you can foul someone.

CALLED FOR CHARGING

Defenders are often the players caught committing fouls. However, an offensive player can get a foul if they play too rough with defenders. If a defender has their feet set and gets bumped by a player with the ball, the offensive player can get called for charging. When that happens, the team on offense must turn the ball over to the other team.

When a player is fouled while trying to shoot, they get to shoot free throws—free shots from the foul line worth one point each. Teams can score a lot of points this way. It's helpful to have players who are good at shooting free throws, and that takes practice!

THINK FAST!

IF A PLAYER GETS A CERTAIN NUMBER OF FOULS, THEY "FOUL OUT," OR HAVE TO LEAVE THE GAME.

Practicing free throws is an important part of playing any position on a basketball team. You never know when you might need to make one!

DIFFERENT IS GOOD

Every basketball player is different, and that means every position can be filled by players of different body types and sizes. For example, some centers are shorter than average, but they're strong enough to do their job well. If you like a certain position, practice the skills you need to become the best you can be at it. That's the most important part!

WHEELCHAIR BASKETBALL

Basketball can be played inside or outside by anyone, well-paid professionals or kids. It can also be played by people who use wheelchairs. Wheelchair basketball is a sport that's part of the **Paralympic Games**. It features five players on each team, and these players move down the court in their wheelchairs.

If you want to learn more, watch the pros in action. Turn on a WNBA or NBA game and see how they shoot, defend, and pass. Knowing the hard work that goes into playing each position makes watching the sport even more fun.

THINK FAST!

COLLEGE BASKETBALL IS A POPULAR SPORT TO WATCH IN THE WINTER AND SPRING. THE SEASON ENDS WITH A TOURNAMENT, OR SERIES OF GAMES, THAT'S OFTEN CALLED MARCH MADNESS.

Basketball is played in many countries around the world. The positions and their jobs are mainly the same no matter where you play the sport.

GLOSSARY

accurately: Done in a way that is free from mistakes; able to hit the target.

asset: A valuable person or thing.

championship: A contest to find out who's the best player or team in a sport.

key: The free throw lane on a basketball court; the lane that extends from underneath the basket to a line 15 feet (4.6 m) in front of the backboard and that players may not enter during a free throw.

opponent: A member of the other team in a game.

Paralympic Games: A series of international sporting contests for athletes with disabilities.

post: The area on a basketball court close to the basket; also known as the paint.

professional: A person who does a job that requires special skill.

react: To do something because of something else that happens.

referee: A sports official who often has final authority in how a game is conducted.

reflex: An action or movement of the body that happens automatically as a reaction to something.

specific: Special or particular.

FOR MORE INFORMATION

BOOKS

Dufresne, Emilie. *Basketball*. New York, NY: KidHaven Publishing, 2020.

Hewson, Anthony K. *Basketball Records*. Lake Elmo, MN: Focus Readers, 2021.

Small, Cathleen. *Basketball*. New York, NY: Gareth Stevens Publishing, 2019.

WEBSITES

Basketball Positions
jr.nba.com/basketball-positions/
The official NBA website has information about all the basic basketball positions.

Hall of Famers
www.hoophall.com/hall-of-famers/
Visitors to this part of the Basketball Hall of Fame website can find short biographies of the game's best players at every position.

WNBA.com
www.wnba.com/
The official WNBA website has information about the league and its players, including what positions its biggest stars play.

Publisher's note to educators and parents: Our editors have carefully reviewed these websites to ensure that they are suitable for students. Many websites change frequently, however, and we cannot guarantee that a site's future contents will continue to meet our high standards of quality and educational value. Be advised that students should be closely supervised whenever they access the internet.

INDEX